INMATES

INMATES

Sean Borodale

CAPE POETRY

1 3 5 7 9 10 8 6 4 2

Jonathan Cape, an imprint of Vintage,
20 Vauxhall Bridge Road,
London SW1V 2SA

Jonathan Cape is part of the Penguin Random House group of companies
whose addresses can be found at global.penguinrandomhouse.com

Penguin
Random House
UK

First published by Jonathan Cape in 2020

penguin.co.uk/vintage

A CIP catalogue record for this book is available
from the British Library

ISBN 9781787331792

Typeset in 11/13 pt Bembo by Jouve (UK), Milton Keynes
Printed and bound in Great Britain by TJ International Ltd, Padstow, Cornwall

Penguin Random House is committed to a sustainable future for
our business, our readers and our planet. This book is made
from Forest Stewardship Council® certified paper.

for Orlando and Louis

written in the presence
of insects living & dying

CONTENTS

INMATES

DEATH PLACE OF A SMALL
TORTOISESHELL UNDER ITS FOOD
SOURCE, THE NETTLE

I am clearing a space.
The billhook I slash with
goes chop.

The effaced sun
streams out a vivid normality.

Do you forget how to look?

It is better, brighter
without being seen.

I can hear it spinning
like a spinning top

as you
die secretly:
a damp mausoleum
of tattered wings.

COMMA BUTTERFLY

It is now past noon;

at the limit of the revolution's height,
a diffuse atomic gloom
burns its dirty flame.

And me, in the microbial
rush, that ticks, ticks,
from the gash I have made

pulling up roots;
the wiring loom
of the underworld's veins surpasses my own.

And there is the soil:
under the dying fall
it boils like dark milk,

as meaningless as a clock,
a trauma, that staples a fractional flow.

Each hour gapes
through the pin-holed bottleneck
at the weltering, the brimming;

it is a wound that crawls.

INSECT EGGS OVER-WINTERING

Here is the sleeping time,
the closed membrane of the egg –
half of eternity's symbiosis.

This is how winter stores its greater proportion,
in preoccupation:
packets of forming anatomy;
cells in patterns almost to patents;
insect of *this*;
the consolation of the unremembered
hidden, hereabouts – in pre-citizenship.

The wind blows cold through the ache of the room.
The room does not ache, of course, it granulates
into the clatter of darkness: plates moved about,
cupboards closed with a hinge,
the tap opened to a cold rushing.

Clap on the need for a light.
It is concentrate, dim.
The aura is eggshell to the darkness it staves off,
violating the ovoid root of each passage;

in voiceless solidarity, its beating edging cell.
Winter; the hunger; the emptying;
adverse beyond yolk sacs
where growing gains self.

HAWK MOTH & QUEEN WASP

In the darkness of woods

a wasp of harried existence
of bitumen and flame;
a moth of flightless troubles,
ash and bracket fungus;

a frugal chase
over balding earths.

I drip with my eyes
to the rupture of one, the plight of the other.

My head is a lump of fist-squeezed clay.

Offer them solidarity – something.
I cannot fly, cannot make sky.

The graft-line between us,
fragile as dry grass before winter rain.

The trees are guts digesting the light.

I do not see the outside of my head;
it is un-mirrored and in abeyance.

BEES & THISTLES

Thistles, three foot, four;
towers of flower-crown, tin shelter,
bleeding black feet;
not any other language, but bleeding feet.
Not collateral or nuance,
but manacled, scratched.
Until it is bees, not thistles,
along edges and tips of sticks;
her intelligence his,
his hers
until end-games of nectaries;
then nothing
but detached wing,
air stained with humming.

MAGGOTS AT THE BACK OF A CUPBOARD

The creepy jewel box
trickles: empty in sound,
but full in score.

How did it start? Each
rice-like, legless maggot:
the two dark hooks of a head.

A life of instars
until the last larval skin
it hammers out of.

The female eyes are apart;
the male's almost touch.
Spongy mouthparts,

all of its frills absorb frail light;
a net-curtain watch
it draws the veil from

at each sharp aggregation, each grope;
aspiring to contact the living
from inside its dead-house.

Eating and egg-life: its séance
nailed into bodies; nailed to swarms
that contract and darken

all surface, to a greasy pale dream
of blowholes and shrapnel;
as in conflict,

emptied and wasted.
Sucked-out hoards of hags;
beggar cases;

wrinkled sheets of the derelict;
sucked into hoover-bags
of use, dis-use;

sucked into fractions
blown out of cities;
sucked out of auras.

BUMBLE BEE

Derelict house.
Three rooms and a thatch.
A grey, tabby pelt.

Red veins on its legs: a fire-red detail.
Staring out to the sky
from its patch of cells.

What help can it give to stare?
But stare.
I have its compatriots:
dry vetch, dry clover.

The blue sky has widened its pupil
to let us through.
The smell of rain is ended.
Corridors of leaf-fall, clattered apart.

The bee's high shoulders are tufted.
Its back, runged like a ladder;
legs preening the body as it had stopped.

The proboscis, where it tapers,
sucks at exhaustion.

BUMBLE BEE: DRY CORPSE

Here are the pulled-glass legs,
smears of pollen:
field-lands of crop that recede
to powder-mould black.

My nerve-lyre mind
is cauterised, too:
a red package of probes
that gets no further than a pang.

Here is the skull, adorned with a fury of hair.
An antlered paralysis;
wings foiling a petroleum sheen of blue.
I am its fall; it transforms me, too,

into moments shielding
a glance
over the sealed shimmer
of a vase that keeps older days.

TICK HATCHERY

Her hatchery

consists of a jam jar.
Set out with tacky, fat-bodied
eggs; iron-brown
helpless contained mass,
the means of new ticks.

After a month, her legs
on the warmest hour
wave over clumped beads that expand,
explode
as the *Popcorn! Popcorn!* of herself.

In the glass jar: the sun magnified,
the fanning legs helpless.

To examine,
to more closely microscope the waiting:
incubating light refracted over clusters
of eggs un-hatched, still.

How she shrinks, and waits and waits over weeks;
attending her helpless, having mothered;
once blood-vast
on old cat's blood or deer blood.

Having birthed or expunged,
she lays, and lives with what she lays,
waterless in the glass jar: prison with vision.

Lit among the dead; air holes above her,
does she hear the vibrating of my approaches
from where mouthed eggs, a house of eggs,
grey, roughed, bedridden weight,
bedlocked, plum-like, lie about her?

Her spinning through the cycle
of gestating days
has succeeded in succeeding:
aloneness is vast.

The sack-body she drags up glass,
once, twice, to slip back,
shrivels as she drinks her interior.

They need of her interior all they can drink.
She finds her part in their thirst.

Grass, soil, microbe; guts, earthen guts,
panning her decay.
Slow fire, clinker of eggs;
fire of passion, if she could find passion.

Somehow passionate,
egg-clusters panning her decay.
The transgression of blood:
soil to grass to rabbit to cat to tick to tick-eggs.

The transgression,
steady in her principle, declines;
her principle steadies to transgression.

She lies up-sided for weeks;
head upturned on its presence,
surrounded by a clottery of eggs.

A ramshackle clutch
that falls, rolls, lies in her slow leg movement
waving upon, or near to the heap, her heap.

Her whole body,
its black battery full of deep red;
a congealing blood-sack,
five weeks old, six weeks old.

What of the tick's interior upon the window,
the single curved pane of the glass jar?

Can she see
when bird sounds, rat sounds,
foot sounds, scurryings,
pass close
and the glass jar solicits a light
containing her irons, her carnage?

It must be one room. It *is* one room.
The lottery of a house, a cell.

Nutrients hardened inside her:
grimy anatomy
seeping up into consciousness.

Destitute of freedom,
she too must clog or go gelatinous;
clawing her prospects, low prospects;
un-birthed pinpricks,
the shrunken crackle of eat-out;

parched beads, burst
blood-stained, blind so far.

Her legs scratch. As tongs to lift.
But none active. None lifted.

All lie quiet.
The hatching un-happened.

DRAGONFLY TRACKING, RE-TRACKING, TRACKING

Spots that it sees, I have seen those too,
in the grimacing light that steals through the woods.

I have seen with its fever, its brittle twitch;
have come to learn its readings;
the way it flies
the double circle of its watch;

glints that instruct: stop, turn, go, take;
sweeping the blurs for recognition.

In the burr of its head,
how long has it lived unseen in water,
to unpack its dry fire's angled music?

By another pond, it may not have lived.

BANDED DEMOISELLE EMERGENCE

Everything has gates, or a door.
The prison is open.

The door into the glare.
Blind within its darkness.

Everything – *everything* – whines and shines.

The moment glares coupled to the moment
the glare is sworn through.

That stick bent or that stick snapped,
what is the difference? A horizontal line:

drawn over a pot,
implies a handle;
around a pit-trap,
serves as a lip.

AUTOPSY OF FUGITIVE ENERGY
FROM A DYING DRAGONFLY

Among alders, willows,
lagged hours of an afternoon;
I lift
a thorax, soundbodymaking;
its background feverfew-green.

The quiet technology of its sashed waist
hides a clock beat.

The injured stump of its tail burns
like metal that cannot cool yet.

A luminous, opaque glaze
that melts at the head.
A surviving scar tissue,
leaks a body leaking.

At the leading edge of each wing
is a quadrangle's
small, dark iron mascot of war:
a hatchet head

I place
on a white sheet of paper;
a somebody/something
nameless and vivid.

How to observe paramedic proximity?
How to co-exist in diagnosis?

You bleed at the mouth
an expenditure I cannot re-supply.

I lift your fugitive, to let you
fall
from the upper storey of the house.
A wing's lily and fermenting pond.
A crash.

As to let a bone out of my own body.
My violent
freedom's final capacity.

PEACOCK BUTTERFLY
COLOUR-WHEEL

A violet cage, a secondary eye;
all that must fly will fly.
Fox fur and rouge; wallflower-red;
a furnace of heat;
dry red of fuller's earth.
Detriment, decayed, the ochre red of caves.
Transparent air,
flecked noise of wing-tremor. Swarf.
A barge's lapped planks caulked with tar.
A pansy's vascular softness.
Primrose glow at dusk.
A bleached poppy's wheel-hub.
A stiff, bog cloth. Glaring sky-blue.
To make its wing and its other wing
true.

WOOD SHED WOOD
PILE INSECTS ROUSED

Guiltily, I go off to write.
Hand-legged, finger-legged,
tiptoe on the ink pen.

I have been at the wood shed.
Rudiments of light. The hut: I built it for wood
to stay in.
Winter is long.

Black gums of last year's leaf mould.
Ash logs,
cherry logs
from a felled tree.

Boreholes, flight holes:
beetle, solitary wasp;
to leave home
it had to eat the walls of its keep.

In light-prism darkness,
cut open the suitcase that carried itself.

What does segue mean?
Yes. Segues
from harbouring to being holed; unharnessed
and vacant; holes from food.

Hard you would think to eat your own walls.
The wooden walls of a cabin.

A slow bullet hole
made by the head.

MAYFLIES UNFINISHED

Bandages of flesh.
Bodies in tourniquet.
Engrossed cupid-white.
Growing towards wings.

Not yet colour; they do not know yet.

They know nothing of flight.
Their bodies know for them.

But I keep watch:
scared;
re-attuned.
Will they turn full-palette,
like a watch
reaching an hour?

Noon is the bleached hour.
Dusk is the time to exist.
The faults cannot be seen at dusk.

I fizz in the woods when I walk.
I think, *this is the nymph*;
I think, *this is me*;
in wood under fungus, in mud under death.

The emergency of the urge to be born.

Nymph-blood beats in my feathered ears.
I will have to learn to create
a shadow from a feel for the air.

It is almost an apprenticeship
to grow under stones.
What will remain?

One thread of me manages.
My lungs stop and they start
like a monastery dinner bell.

It remains to be seen
if I will alarm the air and lift to the sun.

The blue foil of a future day
will arrange me like flowers around a coffin;
a one-day carnage to which plants are invited.

The body causes its own trivia;
its own unmentionables;
distracting an urgency towards sex:

the red fungus of the phallus;
the lips of the dewpond.

I think, *this is it*.

Our babies will be buried, too, in muds
under slow-moving streams;

live colourless, translucent
cot-lives as cold as corpses.

With the defect of a future
that will sometimes be furious.

EFFECT OF A PETROL-ENGINED
LAWN MOWER

Moths rise from the earth.
Bony papers that resurrect lightly.

Blood, so dry it sticks to the mouth.

The sky is a mouth.

The mower's workspace;
its blade-spinning urges them: up, up.

Reflexes deprived of body mass, leak.
What have I done?
Ants drag-work the area. Down again.

Down, down,
into the vaults of their undertow.

Down, into their hospital
of unmentioned anniversaries;
unmarked births.

A social, infallible emergency
they trust to restore.

Ands, and more Ands.

A ground badged with sores.
Down, again. Down.

To re-impregnate; to re-audition;
to re-think earth to harbour eggs.

SIXTEEN HOURS OF A WOOD
WASP ENCOUNTER

Sound-ware of touch:
your silence; except for scratching.

From the side you are different;
quite possibly another altogether.

A woodworker in a brocade dress.
Or in chiffon, a saw held to the ear.
In wing-edge yellows, a lapel; or as cuffs;
the back's bristles ribbed, too.

A thin-waisted woodworker;
a tin-metal face, mapping the unmentionable;
an oil can, because wordless.
Perhaps that is beauty.

Rubbing of the legs, the sores.
Immured
in the laundry of the self.

Then leaning, drinking –
all the effort inside ruckled cloth –
to bend at the lenses of the abdomen.

So far, I have watched a disappearance.
A cask of fatigue,

it could be blown along,
tumbling over
the invisible common, more invisible.

HOUSE FLIES

High summer, the flies are a fog.

One day turns on a tap of flies;
a tap that hatches as it pours
and they scatter up.

My head is their air; their airs sift me.
A loose, elevated physiology.
Who are you?
Winged heads of iron oxide, bulges of bristle.
Sucker-footed, you must be like armies;
a winged rubble
of momentum.
Alert and silicate; a syndicate of littering.
Veined and storm-red, you are like lace;
or electrical circuits bagged up in black nets.

The flies have shorted me.
I burn brightly before I melt
along the fuse of my consciousness.

Better, now that the air sweeps them
slightly to the west of me.

A mechanical ghost of mezzotint and kinetics;
an apparatus of tongue and wind-box,
draining and draining.

It meets me
at the velocity of a psyche,
it drowns what I say.

SLIGHT THREADBARE INSECTS, STILL OPERATIONAL

Holes of riverwater, mineral crumbs;
mould and cellulose;
the honed exteriors of beautiful workers.

The tick, tick tick
of deathwatch courting.

I hear it, first on this side
and then on that.

The hornet regularly swerves up.
When it lands there is a stumped silence.
Over the roof ridge,
where terracotta
is accepting her sound as a jolt of vengeance.

A natural violence

that is a nest shot deep into the
temperature of the head.

A valve of presence
that switches open its stain.
How much I could stain
with the red of my blood.
Nice. But be wary.

They look well in their suits,
flies that cross parables.

BRIMSTONE MOTH, ALIVE

She. As it dies, inhabits
an obfuscated time of isolation.

Primrose and sulphur and yellow hair.

Through the breathing dark house,
fields of stressed air.

She. She carries a torch
to light up the disappeared.

Her sight's bulb, another sight:
rooms ahead of her.

She. She searches the fragile details
of indoors;
the drab, derelict shifts of skyless air.

Who – incomprehensible who –
is crashed out on floors.

The suffering self; as if murdered;
humans, of brindled insides,

dreaming her double;
her double.

BRIMSTONE MOTH, DEAD

I see in the mirror of what saw me –
a microbiology
siphoned off
from the light of the sun.

Quixotic kinetics.
Quiver of leaf over rotten shade.

Under magnification, you become
snipped-up harp.
Pieces swerved into the prismatic.
A magnetic, maniac detail
turbulent with attention.

All touch is mistake;

a breathed, stirred presence
through the cohesive wilds of your hair;
your ordinary,
magnified shreds of infidel.

Where is our commune?

Re-focus; stare at your thorax;
search the bedraggled, yellowed grass;
where the coin of last night's
moon was drowned.

A hole at the heart-place,
round and cold as the disc of a fish-eye.

Who was it left you; like a fairy
leaves money, from another world?

SMALL EMERALD MOTH ALONG
WOOD-ROT

I stagger because sight is a form of stagger.
The closing, wet dampness is short of depth.

I wring out words.
Mouthfuls of sodden speech.

And there they are, fathom-testing the heights.
What has gone wrong with looking?

Greens glisten;
trophies, almost born to be the wet silks of the woods.

Copper earths, veiled with dust;
and dust with dust; defying, managing

broken eternities.

LARVAE, DISTURBED

Born grey:
three quarters web, four fifths web.

Transporting the brain,
the scandal of the brain.

Smelling of the moon,
the coffin-shroud white of the moon.

Gathering the bits,
to hang in the damage.

COBWEB A.M.

Today: gelatine air;
a rig of webs stitched across hedge gaps.

A proletariat of angle-poised limbs
at looms
weaving wheels, which are social.

Everything is the same age in light.

A compass of hunger,
a madrigal of waiting:

they bear the high, wild circle of common, fat
pale block of the morning sun.

Sustained against free-fall,
their futures wait.

I jangle a web to demonstrate life.

At school-time, the car is our spider:
its wheels contract to a web of roads.
We drive miles clocked to the speeds –
all in the average.

At home-time the school bell vibrates.

A predatory, breathless austerity
has waited – . All day,

hours baited with a sticky silence –
for the board and fare of ceasefire.

COBWEB P.M.

Flies inhabit
looped terminals of flight;
defibrillate the death-throe.

The sun flares an astrology of death;
a zodiac of wings;
incendiary, gold; reflected along strings.

A fly hammers the froth
of its final vibrato.

A spider scuttles.
Cancer.
Scorpio.

A death-mouth with silk-threads
on Velcro stilettoes.

You will be liquefied, fly;
within wing-joint and mandible.

She will drink you.

The web is a whiskered hush;
a tensile, panoptic dimension.

She will weave with your power
her wheel of rags, her coiled will.

SPIDER AT MIDWINTER

The shed light, dulled with broken web,
spilt on a scythe-blade's rust.

An argent gleam hangs along a trowel.
A fork's tine speaks but does not move.
A paralysis of ice heals at the window.

Worker hand-marks:
a chafed ash-handle; grease stain,
a cracked plate;
the knocks and scrapes of the utile.

Under the asbestos roof,
the spider's shadow consumes me:
its reddish knuckled pins, crudely perfect.

I cough, and the seed of its body
dilates
into legs: lengths of small sable.

I could paint with one,
its brush-hair delicacy;
repair use-fractures in crockery.

DOUBLE-LOBED MOTH

Here is a black lantern of two parts.
A swollen, split, canister of body.

It says: feel my face,
it is boat-like, drowning; it bleeds black dust.

Up there is the sun.
I am under its terrible power.
My red flecked body, red as garnet.

The four skirts of my devastation
are fumbled apart;
the fungus-grey brackets of my coat,
stuck to my skin.
The silver woods of my underbelly,
bald;
the lace of my winter morning,
torn.
The isometrics of my hospital gown,
slit, and stitched
along the frame of my spine.

The fiction of my birth
behind charcoal lips:
my body of unlearnable moves.

My lighthouse head

crawls into darkness
once every minute.

MOTH INTERCEPTED AND
LOST ON THE BATHROOM WALL

A coin-coloured moth.
I do not think it saw but it knew.

By coin-coloured,
I mean that blackness on copper;
earthgrime of ages in burial.

A republic of interspace
between me and a moth
in the spasm of flicker that is flight.

I walked on legs as dry as plaster
to get to its position.
Where did it go?

All night, the night:
an unlit gauze of ashen darkness, a bodycoat;
the hospital bed of the night where I sleep.

How did I get here,
in a skin as white as a hospital ambulance?

Wake, turn, by fitful energies.
A clock shrieked, shrieking.

They keep me heavy, still, disused;
the indefatigable minutes of life,
the nurses that are time.

Time accomplishes me like the moth.
I am the invalid of time
but that may be a trick.

The moth escaped.
How?
Tumbling through the colour
of a shadow in a corner;

slow and digested through hairpin bends;
the flow of a day, failures of a day.
A distant diaspora.

WOODLOUSE

Grey on the staircase; on fourteen legs.

As rain taps, rattles the window.
Slight turmoil, but safe.

In from waste space the wind agitates
the house.

A crankshaft of hours
turns dark-cold light-cold dark.

This is our place, its entire craft.
But this,

what does it want, the noise?
What does the noise want?

The wind flapping at our edge;
a choice over the other path?

The night's ambience of exaggeration:
born out of tune;
out of tune with sudden choice.

If I move we touch.

What is it like, under your grey shield
of body-plates
you contract to a globe?
A dim wrecking-ball hut
converging in memories of stone-damp,
wood-damp.

I can only imagine
you live like a house.

Only
slow, slower, slowest,
slowly.

CINQUEFOIL TORTRIX
MOTH UNDER GLASS

Gas-mask moon
rising
from a breathed orchestration of damp.

The night pours an inhaling lung
into a small, hard glass of introversion.

Dead slow, dead tired.
Not yet dead of detail,
the details obsess me.

The owl's cry
falls behind trees into octaves of depth,
into deeper
octaves of dimension.

A glass, as small as the moon.

I lower its mouth over the wings.
It amplifies blurring,
ricocheting,
trapped, flared edges trembling.

I watch a particulate snow-fall of scales
drift down seconds
that violently
kick.

I lean at the glass that contains her.

Her copper-filing loops of evening gown,
her neckline filed thin,
her wing-fans sharpened.

She bangs in its cylinder,
and drops, and bangs again;
blurred
in the rictus of a damaged flight.

BITS OF A GREY HAWK MOTH
CEMENTED TOGETHER

Under a flapping, dark thin plane
of wings;
a drawer of taut stiffened cloth; rigor mortis
hovering
in the shadow of the shadow of the room around the floor.

Ash — nothing that weighs very much;
nothing but ash; molecules;

the impediment of a mound
that is
unfallen ash, latched to a hinge.

Auto-symmetry. Born so.
Trembling, troubled.

A moth psyche
enduring the fungal time-creep of woods;
closure of light;
the dimming, bright gland of the air,

all the way back — to Aristotle;

the lines of a prison that moves its bars;
made endurable, wearable:
life gravely worn.

Before the moon brings difficulties
that need waiting out.

When blood rockets through its filters.
When the battered rest.

WHITE PLUME MOTH

A moth waits, in the kitchen's
aspic of shadow,
folded; not calling for help.
All day, no difference.

Its tarpaulin laces, unclasped;
it carries a piece of the mist
flooded with moonlight;
a plug of the moon in its face.

The pellets of its eyes
see me seeing it

scull,
almost alone.
Its hull's snow-white
is a summer snow.

GRASSHOPPER

If I sit still for long enough
insects land on me.

The key-change
is the landing of the grasshopper.

Taut-backed, antennae back-swept;
file-teeth rasp its sprung energy.
The leap, its field-song's parabola.

The rough river's emeralds are in the grasses,
luminous as light-echoes through seeding cores.
Cobalt emission; gelatinous scarlet.

Lunatic as a match-strike or electric switch
in a hall of gas,
living by intervals.

And then, it extinguishes total speed,
rewinding all trigger to stopping still.

Its blood-red strings catch it, internally.

LADYBIRD (DEAD ON A LAMPSHADE)

It takes months, years,
to seal a biography:

a shawl of dust,
a closure of self.

My own dust is there;
other inhabitants, too,
have conflated skin, towel,
dead body-tissue.

A ladybird's shell:
a car shut down
under snowfall.

A car that has waited
too long to be rescued.

Two metal-snipper wings
protrude at the back:

doors of an old
Volkswagen body

that mimicked freedom,
that petered out.

SHIELD BUG EXAMINED IN
BITTER GREEN

A velocity:
which bears the diamond of a green banner;
the protest
of an alone I

marked with its body.

As if in climbing,
it can reach the cleft between clicks
of the second hand of the clock.

Its squared tail-sheath,
a broken key;
walking up over the vertical of the clock
that ticks.

Carrying a green jar of carborundum paste
with which to grind
the cog-edge of time to a smooth plane.

The milk grey fluff of the human
caught in its legs.

What will it do with such a green triangle,
a set of faces?

Wing veins in overlap.
Wings that do not fly.

I watch with nerves
at the gate of the jump that leaps the room apart.

Were you born, or made?

A soundless, copious singularity,
digesting a path.

CRICKETS AND NOISE OF
GRASSES AND PERSEIDS

The vault of night lifts overhead.
I can hear
streaked light too fast to interrupt,

can feel the friction of a meteor;

crickets
setting out nodes, that will constellate later.

Under the helmet of dawn,
their milliseconds will strike.

There is nothing tentative.
The cold fever
cannot accomplish heat.

What am I lying in?
A body, breathing.
A sharpening that pins me to the boards of the table:
saw-chafed and frozen.

The cloth I wear
is made of listening to my skin.

I smell the damp dead-grass;
a saturated decay of dripping woods,
nearer than my blood.

I breathe to rescue ruined air.

Earth moves.
I am not afraid of being broken, or hit.

My dry bones will make a sound;
their snaps will configure

the spasm of a future.

PALE GESTATING CENTIPEDES
UNDER ROTTING BARK OF
STACKED CHERRY WOOD

Split a wet log, an alligator log,
to reveal
a flattened life between iron hooks.
Homeless. Of a sudden. Ruined.

Furs are snagged among thistle spurs,
shards of hogweed;
the failing grasses, breathed across.

Here is a skeleton.
I think in its ossuary.
Each thought is a dry bone, a slow calm.
The odd singular one
is hurrying on crotchety legs.

That must be something I haven't invented:
centipedes
fattening under rotten tree-bark in the woods.

The moon is quivering
on a square of trembling wet.

A closed-down, harrowing quiet begins.
The decayed, devastated annuities of trees.
The collapsing quoits of years.
What survives this

in milk-clothed flesh,
downstairs in the self?
To re-investigate the world;
in soft, web-silks to contain new hunger?

Here is a body's pip;
a released spine; a solipsist
of complication.

It siphons and slinks
quicker than writing;
but disturbed, unripe.

WATER ERMINE MOTH COMING
OUT OF THE DARK

In everything, the slow allegory of slowness.
Moth, still; scroll-wing, slow; lacewing, stopped.

Sods of light, when the light is switched on;
sods
thrown from the window
onto grass below.

(Window of splaying light-cast.)

Moth that drinks, stills, lists
at drinking. Stops.

The night-edge of the slow creases of water;
squeak of shrew:
slower vibration, it thunders.

Turn a right angle: you can,
it exists
in the going from a room to another.

But turn, to catch the bright bead of the eye
indexed at palest amethyst.
Or rose quartz, perhaps.

A chink from the eye of a cat.
A small chip of partiality, sinking forever.

A moth's ghost, from as far away as Saturn.

Weak torchlight
signals through vast interference;

too slowly amber to be caught
as it falls
through a slow, deep pool of hours

(water dishevels
to drink it, dimly)

who falls
with its torch beam left awake.

A moth inside the shadows of the woods.
Of mottled stare.
A triangle, contorted by wing tremor.
A torn scrap of total dark.
Rain spots on rosehips.
Cockle-shell, bone-white; mollusc-black.
Fuselage of bodice silks, weasel furs
that tinkle with a silver globular dew.
Rain spittle, a mouth horn that murmurs.
Milk-mouthed, mealy-eared.
Powder-coated; electrolysis of earth.

WOOD SHED SPIDER WITH
CLOTH OF OTHERS

Spiders in the woodpile
we will burn to make heat.

The drowned earth's damp,
the lowered evenings
into sudden dark.
Hurling through the winter in our walls;
housed if lucky.
Hurled into thunderbolts of snow.

I lift one log, webbed with a tacky silk.
Cotton-flock sacks of inside grain;
creeping organs of presence.

Shifts body under cloth.
Pulses or reacts.

So earthed its iron is endowed with magnetics;
its coppers with charge,
its silicates with flow.

Lives in the marrow of wooden hearts
we will burn to make heat.

What does a beetle burn like?
Its flame a shroud, tiny, flapping
in the mass of its bigger house-fire.

I did not mean to burn you, too.
I forgot,
wood is not pure.

DEVIL'S COACH HORSE BEETLE

Sleekly, it judders
the midwinter house's night's
oppressive, staved, singular space.

The rest of the world is forgotten.
This is the place, the only place.

The sound of scurrying, tapping.
Do you hear it? Do you answer?

The cold window
snagged with condensation:
a convex, shielding headstone of glass.

I earn my minutes of survival
staying awake
to see how others survive me.

Clocksilence.
The last ticking erased.
The unwound clock, ceased.

Something at its heart, this room;
something that has eaten the world.

A trapped minute's stillness
at which the beetle crosses;

inhabitant in all space, all time,
along a path that has left words,
left years in words to survive them.

DEVIL'S COACH HORSE BEETLE SLOWLY THROUGH A MOMENT OF WITNESS

Even here, its artery is of black silence
juddering over painted concrete
of the kitchen floor.

A silent siren,
carrying a consequence of its entering.
The beetle articulates furiously, on.

Time, so still so thickened
I cannot cross it after it
but hold it

opening across me,
closing across me.

Is it a kinship?
What will I do with an 'us' that absorbs me?

Have I mentioned the barbs,
the fringed bristles along the legs,
the segments of antennae?
The prismatic sheen across blackness?
Each part immaculate;
un–bruised, un–chafed as something born.

No.
But in the slow whirlpool of the room:
to have passed a beetle on nearly equal terms.

DRINKER MOTH

Beautiful moth: it dream-shivers
along a lake of night, a coast.
A black square of opened window.

The curls of its antennae:
ram-horned brush-strokes of bright mineral.

A white spot, pale as the gullet of a trout.
A black eye, small as a knot of black thread.

It is trickling
a smoothed external calibre of thought
in pheromone.

Here is a piece of Aschenputtel, but male
in sections of satin light;
a weft of trembling.

What is so urgent it suspends flight?
In mildew-smelling air,
in urine and mould,

to be male under an inner moon;
raining a power off the body
like dry, red earth falling from a plane.

What is so urgent it must start again?

Cracking in agitation wood-shaving wings.
Scattering symmetry through a blur of thrashes
along edges of trees.

Until it rests: a brown tent of two wings;
its pen-tipped goblin-face
protruded, absorbing the rain.

Its throat, fragile as rose petals.

But what *is* the choice,
for a psyche; a cupid of wrestling?

One that is copied
from one second to the next:

smaller, weaker; smaller and weaker.

FLIES, STARTING & STOPPING

Meadowsweet is frothing over water.
All of the colours are of off-stage events:

the dragonfly perched on a dropwort leaf
was earlier hunting in sunset yellows;

the orange-tip, fluttering,
was recently poised into egg-laying
under the candyfloss pink of a cuckooflower.

The gelatinous festering pond edge:
the sound, a colour —
a brushed diaphanous pain
smeared through the flesh of air.

An intensity in listening
complicated, fraught,
at odds and in rhyme with the multitudinous,
gelatinous festering edge.

The flies are in flux.

The music sweeps them.
The music stops.

VOICE RESIDUE OF A MAYFLY AT THE SITE OF ITS EMPTY EXOSKELETON

How far should I go?

In the canopy of my new skin;
no family, no bloodline.
I find I must borrow.

The water I was made of
swims through my blood.
The heart hangs like river shadow,
dripping from its weight.
Silks.
Stones.
Objects of the forest river.
Where I was born
and born backwards again out of my mouth
into haze and sweet airs.
Leaving the shadow of a black-outlined boat
of glass planks of wood.

Sunlight is like a nurse
who crunches back and forth raking me through a gravel of glass.

The marquee of my world,
quartz plates, or sheets: a body skin.

What does the water want?
Or the light?

Only to dismantle what was first borrowed.

For the mouth of memory
has no body.

A GLANCE THROUGH AIRBORNE
PARTICLES & INSECTS

I watch, as I watch, have watched before.
Look up,
through aqueous thickness,
at gelatinous motes,
at harpooned microbiologies,
at corsets of flights unlaced.
I trail a hand, but it reaches nothing.
I see that the laws, the risks,
are being lived,
making of their agility their love.

Angels of chainsaw-oil and sparks;
of fish-fleshed airs
that hang in the woods in slivers;
beating flecked panes of flesh.
Whatever these are, they move
through couplings:
a livid numeracy,
a median of metabolisms;
a fog of flight-ware
being tried, being used.

MIGRANT HAWKER DRAGONFLY: WITH LILIES FOR WINGS IT ATTEMPTS

Incoherences distil in my eyes
until seeing is planar, replete; vanished
of obstacles, obstinacies;
traverses more possible.

What will you make of me?

The grown trickles of chemicals;
the sulphur hidden, the magnesium hidden,
the potassium, sodium?

My water has absorbed what it needs.
The flicker of a symptom
swerves.
A reverb hangs over grass blades.

Listen. Twitch.
Tappets.
The air's camshaft shimmers
a wobble of stars.

Warm, I am an engine
on a stretcher.
I forget
I can still fly.

MAYFLY DAY

Stare at its single black eye.
It is going up.

It has found neck-ache
by trying to live.

The scratch achieves it a death.
A pin-prick of blood.

Quite simple to stop,
for it is spent.

Air moves as a hearse
in and out of the coach-house of the mouth.

It worries about the broken mirror
of the earth's imagination

as it falls to vapour,
and turns back to stone.

Blotting it, rain hooks
a calcite cloak over its back:

an alabaster coat,
a fat small frock of water.

Water cobwebs in its sockets.

Flight draws it, like an egg
sucked from its shell.

A posthumous wound.
A faceted abandonment.
The sound of a curtain.

The light is a posy of dried monsters.
A halo of sun
browned to a feathered ring.
Revolt, caught into a tambourine.

There are its wings:
they shake to a hush;

sweeping its desiccated, wrecked state
out.

HOT BRIGHT VISIONARY FLIES

The hot lozenge lifts.
Up-risings; downfalls.
A ticking beyond sound.
A red square of falling sun.

A mass breathing, beating.

A sky, studded with stones
fraught with cut light.
An abolished mechanics
at dewdrop scale:

onyx, topaz, opal.
Each a dull pulsing.

One day, it will stop:
the air will stop; the light will stop.

ACKNOWLEDGEMENTS

Thanks due to the editors of the *Guardian*, *Irish Times*, *New Humanist Review*, *Oxford Poetry*, *POEM International*, *Poetry Review*, *Dispatches*. I have been lucky to hold fellowships which have enriched the development of this book, and so thanks to: Oscar Wilde Centre, Trinity College Dublin, in particular Chris Morash and Aileen Douglas; the Moore Institute, NUI Galway and Daniel Carey; the Clandeboye Estate, Lady Dufferin and Jane Ohlmeyer; the Santa Maddalena Foundation and Beatrice Monti della Corte. Thanks to Poetry Ireland and to Arts Council England. Thanks also to Tim Dee, Jennifer Clement, James L. Hayes, Lionel Pilkington and John Kenny for rallying the spirit; to Carol Ann Duffy for eternal support and for making her last laureate reading a protest of poems and poets against declining insect populations; and not least, to my editor, Robin Robertson. Great thanks to Steve Boyland for discourse and collaboration on 'the lyrigraph sessions' which stand behind these pieces as an exploratory theatre of writing, reading, sounding, utterance. Thanks to Kelsey Hennegen for taking the time to read and to respond. Especial thanks to Jane Borodale, and to Orlando and Louis to whom this book is dedicated, who knew and shared the house with the many life-forms on and for which these pieces were written. Especial thanks to Kathryn Maguire for being lodestar and light. Gratitude to so many writers, artists, activists, scientists, custodians of place and spirit who have taken the plight of insects and everything meshed and connected with them (which is like everything) as their cry and concern; to all who have opened, awakened and agitated my own attempts to reach ways of voice as marks on a page. These 'poems' were written in the same locality as *Bee Journal*, *Human Work*, *Asylum*, and likewise grew from earlier screen-printed, performed, situated writings called 'lyrigraphs'. Thank you to the place and all its inhabitants; deepest gratitude to the insects.